I0490830

When
Self-Motivation
Is dead...

Where do you draw your strength from?

By

Oluyemi Stephen Beloved

Published in Nigeria by:

Evangelist Oluyemi Stephen Beloved Ministries.

Plot 3, Aanuoluwapo community Omisanjana.

Ado, Ekiti State. Nigeria.

+2348062482454, +2348067031214

oluyemistef@gmail.com

Dedication:

This book is dedicated to my Christian's brothers and sisters all over the world who are tired, frustrated and confused.

I also specifically dedicate this book to my young brother, Master Daramola Oluwadarasimi Ife.

I wrote you this letter to ignite your passion, awake the willingness in you to encourage yourself to carry on with the good works.

PREFACE:

Life has dual phases. Where there is good there must of necessity be a bad side. This generic assumption gives all little children the idea that God is associated with white colour, light and good things whereas, dark colour, darkness and all manner of evil atrocities signalled the Devil.

I have also experienced two sides of life like you. We have shared a moment of joy and of sadness. We had all tasted the moment of excitement and a memory full of dull moment.

In our journey, we have seen speed and tumbling. At times we have things going on smoothly and fine with us until we all reached that junction, the juncture of weariness and lack of motivation to continue in the good work.

In Christ body, the faithful brethren called this junction a spiritual light out. At the junction where you began to feel that it is meaningless to stick to the goal which gives you the idea that you stand to gain nothing; or perhaps you loss interest in all reasons to continue. It's not uncommon here to see self-motivation been replaced with boredom, dryness, moodiness etc.

The scriptures in **Hebrew 10: 24 - 25** shall be the mirror of truth for this article. The Bible says *"And let us consider how we may spur one another on toward love and good deeds.*

Let us not give up meeting together, as some are in the habit of doing, but let us encourage one another and all the more as you see the Day approaching."

ToC:

Chapter 1

Dealing with Lack of Self Motivation

Lack of self motivation is a common issue that many people face in their lives. It can be a major obstacle to achieving personal, professional, and even our heavenly race goals. If you are struggling with a lack of motivation, it is important to understand the causes and symptoms of this issue, as well as ways to overcome it.

So, first thing to do now is to take a pen and try to make a list of known causes of distractions in your life. On another page make a list of things you know is not making you to stay awake to actions, things killing your will of doing things you are supposed to do or carry on with the mission ahead. Finally, make a list of what you think or learnt much later that you could have done differently to be vibrant, fervent and strong in faith. This will be your end result at the end of this study.

I will give few examples of common things that have led to partial and in some cases total loss of self-motivation which had made many to quit faith/ heavenly race or in your case it maybe yielding to a fierce persuasion to make you take it slow.

Remember **Galatians 5: 6 – 10.**

> *"For* **in Christ Jesus** *neither circumcision nor uncircumcision has any value.* **The only thing that counts is faith expressing itself through love.**
>
> *You were running a good race. Who cut in on you and kept you from obeying the truth?*
>
> *That kind of persuasion does not come from the one who calls you.*
>
> *'A little yeast works through the whole batch of dough.'*
>
> *I am confident in the Lord that you will take no other view. The one who is throwing you into confusion will pay the penalty, whoever he may be."*

Causes of Lack of Self Motivation

As explained above there are many different factors that can contribute to a lack of self motivation. Some common causes include:

1. **Fear of Failure**: When you are afraid of failing, it can be difficult to find the

motivation to take action. You may worry that you will not succeed, so you avoid taking risks or trying new things.

The word of God has your backing here. If you leap you will rise. *See* **Daniel 11:32** *"... but the people that know their God, they shall be strong and do exploit."*

The Lord frowns at cowards - the lazy cows as Americans call them. God does not want His own heritages to be lazy or fearful. We read the word "**fear not**" in the Bible 365 times. Meaning in all the 365 days that make a year, God is with us all through. So, my friend, stop this procrastination. There is a wise saying, whatever worth doing at all is worth doing well. That business idea you are so afraid of starting, God is with you just start and you will thank Him.

In **2 Timothy 1: 7** we read *"For God hath not given us the spirit of fear; but of power, and of love, and of a sound mind."* Whenever the fear of failure is discouraging you and killing the good motivation in you, I want you to say this loud to yourself in front of a standing mirror, I am not wired to fail. I cannot fail. I am not afraid. I have sound mind. I am in my right senses. I may make mistakes but I am not a failure. I am continuing strong and winning in Jesus name. Amen. Hallelujah!

Wow! What a relief! You just start with the first step today. Listen, if anyone tells you that you have failed. Fire it back at him/her that sorry sir I am not a failure and I cannot fail. This one you see is just a mistake and I can fix it. See each failure as a correctable mistake. You will end well in Jesus name.

2. **Lack of Clarity:** If you are unsure about what you want to achieve or how to get there, it can be hard to find the motivation to take action. Without a clear goal or plan, you may feel like you are spinning your wheels and not making progress.

I John 7: 4 *"No one who wants to become a public figure acts in secret. Since you are doing these things, show yourself to the world."*

Habakkuk 2: 2 *"Then the LORD replied: 'Write down the revelation and make it plain on tablets so that a herald may run with it. For the revelation await an appointed time; it speaks of the end and will not prove false. Though it linger, wait for it; it will certainly come and will not delay."*

Understanding your life goals, making it plain, that is, packaged it in such a way that others can run with it will give you public announcement without paying for adverts.

3. **Burnout**: If you are overworked, stressed, and exhausted, it can be hard to find the energy and motivation to tackle new challenges. Burnout can leave you feeling depleted and unmotivated.

If this explains your present condition, don't worry. Simply read as loud as possible to yourself the book of **Ecclesiastes 7: 8 NCV** *"It is better to finish something than to start it. It is better to be patient than to be proud."*
I want you to turn it to inharmonious song. Sing I must finish what I started because I am better than the best.

4. **Negative Self-Talk:** If you constantly criticize yourself and doubt your abilities, it can be hard to find the confidence and motivation to pursue your goals. Negative self-talk can undermine your self-esteem and make it difficult to take action.

The Bible says the power of life and death is in the tongue. **Proverbs 18:21 AMP** *"Death and life are in the power of the tongue, and those who love it and indulge it will eat its* *fruit and bear the consequences of their words."* Now you see, anything that goes out of your mouth either good or bad will come back to affect you. That's the power of the released or spoken words.

==============================

However, the excitement you once had to complete well, to finish the heavenly race strong in glory and/or to accomplish a task does not and cannot just fade away overnight. There is gradual process to loosing fervency. Long time unchecked loss of passion, zeal or interest could lead to death to self-motivation to carry out expected mission goals.

Symptoms of Lack of Self Motivation

If you are experiencing a lack of self - motivation, you may notice some of the following symptoms:

1. **Procrastination**: If you find yourself putting off tasks or avoiding them altogether, it may be a sign that you are lacking motivation.
2. **Lack of Energy:** If you are feeling tired and lethargic, it can be hard to find the motivation to take action.

3. **Lack of Interest:** If you are no longer interested in the spiritual exercises – the things you used to enjoy, it may be a sign that you are experiencing a lack of motivation.

4. **Negative Thoughts:** If you are constantly thinking negative thoughts and doubting yourself, it can be hard to find the motivation to pursue your goals. See **Romans 12: 2 NIV,** *"Do not conform any longer to the pattern of this world, but be transformed by the renewing of your mind. Then you will be able to test and approve what God's will is-his good, pleasing and perfect will."*

Ways to Overcome Lack of Self Motivation

I wrote this letter to help you stay motivated during difficult times. Motivation is a key factor in achieving success and happiness in life, so it's important to find ways to maintain it even when things get tough. Here are some tips that may help:

1. **Set clear goals:** Having clear, specific goals can help you stay focused and motivated. Make sure your goals are achievable and measurable, and break them down into smaller, more manageable steps.

See **Habakkuk 2:1-3, Jeremiah 12:5** says *'If you have raced with men on foot and they have worn you out, how can you compete with horses? If you stumble in safe country, how will you manage in the thickets by the Jordan?*

If you don't understand yourself and your life goals, nobody will understand you. You cannot afford to run backwards and not confuse the world.

2. **Find your why:** Knowing why you're doing something can give you a sense of purpose and help you stay motivated. Take some time to reflect on your values and what's important to you, and use that as motivation to keep going.

> **Psalms 49: 20** "*Man that is in honour, and understandeth not, is like the beasts that perish.*"

Why are you gifted with that position and what's the expectation of the giver? Be it from God or humanity you must know what is expected of you and why you must not fail.

This is a source of inspiration you can draw your strength from.

3. **Celebrate small wins**: Celebrating small victories can help you stay positive and motivated. Take time to acknowledge your progress and give yourself credit for the hard work you're putting into your project.

The value you place on your achievements and the people coming to join you to celebrate are real sources of inspiration too. The only exception to this is if it is ministry. You are to turn that feeling of celebration to thanksgiving and a way to win more souls to God. You don't throw party for building a church cathedral or for healing the sick. That's because they are not intellectual ability or our work. You can't take praise or credit over someone else's work. Hence, Apostle Paul asked *was it not Jesus that died.* So let's give him credit for what he perfected.

However, if you do something differently, and reach a mile stone, I don't think there is a crime in it to invite friends, colleagues and family to celebrate you while you are still alive.

Ecclesiastes 5: 18 *"Behold that which I have seen: it is good and comely for one to eat and to drink, and to enjoy the good of all his labour that he taketh under the sun all the* *days of his life, which God giveth him: for it is his portion.*

vs19. *Every man also to whom God hath given riches and wealth, and hath given him power to eat thereof, and to take his portion, and to rejoice in his labour; this is the gift of God.*

vs20. *For he shall not much remember the days of his life; because God answereth him in the joy of his heart."*

4. **Surround yourself with positivity:** Surrounding yourself with positive people and influences can help you stay motivated and focused. Seek out friends and mentors who support your goals and inspire you to be your best self.

When I was single and was provided with the privilege to pastor a church, I did two things that made people fear and hated me initially but when they began to see the results they changed their minds and started to copy it till today. The first thing was to select 4 boys in junior class I called them sons of prophets. They live with me; train with me and fast with me. The second thing is I forbid opposite sex access to my house. It was written on my door "no entrance to anyone in skirt, blouse or gown". I fenced away opposite sex completely. When I am in the church to counsel, minister or do whatever doable, these sons of prophet are always there with me.

They were so strict and committed that people begin to seek them for permission to see me. When I am attending to opposite sex, the moment she stands up and close in on me, the sons of prophets grab her and throw her to prayer room where the deliverance squad are angrily ready to deal with all fowl spirits in such people.

It became impossible for any of them to defile or despise my youth. I am not asking you to do the same but I am sharing with you what worked for me several years ago. I left the pastoring job of the church with clean record.

Why was it possible? I recognized the facts that prophetic gifts attract emotional feeling and lusts. As long as I want to continue operating to the best capacity, I have to build a positive atmosphere for myself. I did and it worked. I don't believe that the gift and power of God keep any man of God from sex. In fact, the more gifted and anointed you are the more susceptible to immorality you become. Anointing announces men. Women are angrily waiting for a man who stands out among the rest. Hence, the ugly phenomena we are reading now about increasing falling rate of men of God. Lots of which comes from overconfident.

To stay motivated, inspired and on fire to do good things you are called to do, you must build a like minded and knowledgeable people around your life. Read **Psalms 1: 1-2.**

5. **Take care of yourself:** Taking care of your physical, spiritual and mental health is essential for maintaining motivation. Make sure you're getting enough sleep, eating well, exercising regularly, and taking time for self-care and relaxation. And to stay spiritually alerted and strong you must never joke with quiet time where you can build you devotional life.

Remember, staying motivated is a journey, and it's okay to have setbacks and obstacles along the way. The important thing is to keep moving forward and to never give up on your goals and dreams.

Also, we will all come to a time where we will be faced with rejection. When this happens it's like a sledgehammer just landed on our skull. At this juncture, many fell down and loose it. If you have reached this level what must you do?

Chapter 2

HOW TO HANDLE REJECTION

←—————————————————→

"I took you from the ends of the earth; from its farthest corners I called you. I said, 'You are my servant' I have chosen you <u>and have not rejected you</u>."
Isaiah 41: 9 NIV.

Being rejected by someone you love can be one of the most painful experiences in life. It can leave you feeling hurt, sad, and confused. Rejection is a normal part of the human experience, but that doesn't make it any less painful. In this article, we'll discuss the causes of rejection, the dangers of loneliness, and what to do to overcome moodiness and rejection. We'll also highlight steps to repair a broken relationship.

Job 22:29 ERV

"When people are brought down and you ask God to help them, he will rescue those who have been humbled."

When you as a church member are suffering from rejection, it can be a difficult experience to navigate. As a Christian, it is important to turn to the Bible for guidance on how to handle rejection. Here are some points to consider:

1. Remember that rejection is not unique to you.

Rejection is a common experience that many people go through. In fact, the Bible reminds us that even Jesus faced rejection during his time on earth. In **John 1:11**, it is written, *"He came to his own, and his own people did not receive him."* This verse serves as a reminder that rejection is not a reflection of our worth or value. It's neither the results of our sins nor because of the sins of our parents.

2. Trust in God's plan.

When we are rejected, it can be easy to become discouraged and lose sight of God's plan for our lives. However, it is important to remember that God has a purpose for everything that happens in our lives, including rejection. **Romans 8: 28** says, *"And we know that in all things God works for the good of those who love him, who have been called according to his purpose."* This verse reminds us that God can use even the difficult experiences in our lives for our ultimate good.

3. Don't let rejection define you.

It is important not to let rejection define who we are as individuals. Instead, we should focus on our identity in Christ. In **1 Peter 2:9**, it is written, *"But you are a chosen people, a royal priesthood, a holy nation, God's special possession, that you may declare the praises of him who called you out of darkness into his wonderful light."* This verse reminds us that we are loved and valued by God, and that our identity is rooted in Him.

4. Choose forgiveness.

When we are rejected, it can be easy to hold onto bitterness and resentment towards those who have hurt us. However, as Christians, we are called to forgive others, just as Christ has forgiven us. In **Colossians 3:13**, it is written, *"Bear with each other and forgive one another if any of you has a grievance against someone. Forgive as the Lord forgave you."* This verse reminds us that forgiveness is a key part of our Christian walk, and that it can help us to move past the pain of rejection.

****

In summary, when facing rejection as a Christian, it is important to remember that we are not alone. We can turn to the Bible for guidance on how to handle rejection, trusting in God's plan, focusing on our identity in Christ Jesus.

Causes of Rejection

There are many reasons why someone might reject you. It could be because they don't feel the same way or they are not ready for a relationship. It could also be because of something you did or said that turned them off. Some people may reject you because of their own issues, such as fear of intimacy or commitment.

It's important to remember that rejection is not always about you. It's often a reflection of the other person's feelings, thoughts, and experiences. It's important to try not to take it personally and to focus on moving forward.

One skit maker said, "I hate it when people walk out of my life. I actually want them to run out". His statement meant a lot to me. I see a matured heart that had learnt to accommodate and handle well without prejudice the shocks of rejection.

Now you see I want you to grow up.

Dangers of Loneliness

After a rejection, it's common to feel lonely and isolated. Loneliness is a dangerous emotion that can lead to depression, anxiety, and other mental health issues. It's important to take steps to combat loneliness and to stay connected with friends and family.

One way to combat loneliness is to take up a new hobby or interest. This can help you meet new people and build new connections. It's also important to stay active and to get plenty of exercise. This can help improve your mood and reduce feelings of loneliness.

Also, attend fellowship of Christian brethren, dance away your sorrows and fill your heart with joy in worship. This can also help you really well.

What to Do to Overcome Moodiness and Rejection?

It's normal to feel moody and emotional after a rejection. However, it's important to take steps to manage these feelings and to avoid getting stuck in a negative cycle.

One way to manage moodiness and rejection is to practice self-care. This includes getting enough sleep, eating a healthy diet, and engaging in activities that bring you joy e.g. praise and worship, playing instruments etc. It's also important to talk to someone about your feelings, whether it's a friend, family member, your pastor or a therapist.

Another way to overcome moodiness and rejection is to focus on personal growth. This could mean taking a class or learning a new skill. It could also mean setting goals for yourself and working towards them.

Finally, try pure Christianity. It teaches us to remove our hearts from worldly things, never covet the achievements of unbelievers and to never be worried about what to eat, put in or money to spend. True Christianity teaches us to live with future | eternity in mind.

Steps to Repair a Broken Relationship

Repairing a broken relationship that was caused by rejection can be challenging, but it is possible with effort and commitment from both parties. Here are some steps that can be taken to repair such a relationship, along with relevant Bible verses:

1. ***Acknowledge the problem and take responsibility for your actions***. This includes admitting to any hurtful behaviour or words that may have caused the rejection.

> *"Confess your sins to each other and pray for each other so that you may be healed." -* ***James 5:16.***

2. ***Seek forgiveness from the other person***. This involves expressing sincere remorse for your actions and asking for their forgiveness.

> *"Be kind to one another, tender-hearted, forgiving one another, as God in Christ forgave you." -* ***Ephesians 4:32.***

3. ***Communicate openly and honestly with each other.*** This includes listening attentively to the other person's perspective and expressing your own thoughts and feelings in a respectful manner.

*"Let your speech always be gracious, seasoned with salt, so that you may know how you ought to answer each person." - **Colossians 4:6.***

4. **Work to rebuild trust**. This involves being consistent in your words and actions, and following through on any promises you make.

> *"Let what you say be simply 'Yes' or 'No'; anything more than this comes from evil." - **Matthew 5:37.***

5. **Be patient and persistent**. Healing a broken relationship takes time and effort, but with commitment and perseverance, it is possible to restore the relationship.

> *"And let us not grow weary of doing good, for in due season we will reap, if we do not give up." - **Galatians 6:9.***

Note: A marriage or relationship that God will not fix, no man can fix it, just walk away.

Ultimately, repairing a broken relationship requires humility, honesty, forgiveness, and a willingness to work towards reconciliation. With God's help and guidance, it is possible to heal even the most broken of relationships.

Q: What to do if things you have passed through in life is now hunting you and will not be erased from your mind?

Chapter 3

DEALING WITH ANXIETY

Anxiety is a common and normal emotion experienced by everyone from time to time. It is a feeling of unease, such as worry or fear, which can be mild or severe. While it is normal to feel anxious in certain situations, excessive and persistent anxiety can be a sign of an anxiety disorder.

Some warning signs of anxiety can include excessive worry or fear, restlessness, irritability, difficulty concentrating, and physical symptoms such as sweating, palpitations, and muscle tension. Anxiety can also lead to avoidance behaviors, where individuals avoid situations or activities that may trigger their anxiety. The worst of it all is unconscious worry. It is difficult to diagnose. Yet, it results in high blood pressure.

Fortunately, there are ways to manage and overcome anxiety. One effective method is through cognitive-behavioral therapy (CBT), which helps individuals identify and change negative thought patterns and behaviors that contribute to their anxiety. Relaxation techniques such as deep breathing, meditation, and progressive muscle relaxation can also be helpful in reducing anxiety.

Additionally, lifestyle changes such as regular exercise, a healthy diet, and adequate sleep can improve overall mental health and reduce anxiety symptoms. In some cases, medication may also be prescribed by a healthcare professional to help manage anxiety.

While anxiety is a normal emotion, excessive and persistent anxiety can be a sign of an anxiety disorder. It is important to recognize the warning signs of anxiety and seek help if necessary. With the right tools and support, it is possible to manage and overcome anxiety and improve overall mental health and well-being.

What is the best remedy to anxiety? I will say rest in God. Trust in His all-surpassing grace and inevitable promises. Be anxious for nothing.

CAST YOUR CARES ON GOD

1 Peter 4:7-8

*"**4:7.** The end of all things is near. Therefore <u>be clear-minded</u> and self-controlled so that you can pray.*

__4:8.__ Above all, love each other deeply, because love covers over a multitude of sins."

Life is full of desires. We are wired to desire.

Desire in itself is actually legitimate.

The problem however is when such desire is becoming anxiety and worries.

- Desires cannot run by itself freely.
- It requires human heart to run.
- It is however dangerous to allow it to run through us non check.
- The more it runs freely the more injurious it becomes.
- Once we allow it to become worries and anxiety it begins to frustrate and that's a problem.

Biblical advice

Gal. 5: 26, Matthew 6:31-32. I Peter 5:7.

Galatians 5: 26-27 | *"Since we live by the Spirit, let us keep in step with the Spirit. Let us not become conceited, provoking and envying each other."*

Matthew 6: 31-34| *"So do not worry, saying, 'What shall we eat?' or 'What shall we drink?' or 'What shall we wear?' For the pagans run after all these things, and your heavenly Father knows that you need them. But seek first his kingdom and his righteousness, and all these things will be given to you as well. Therefore do not worry about tomorrow, for tomorrow will worry about itself. Each day has enough trouble of its own."*

1 Peter 5: 6-7 | *"Humble yourselves, therefore, under God's mighty hand, that he may lift you up in due time. Cast all your anxiety on him because he cares for you."*

A food for thought: a wise one once said, you cannot stop a bird from flying but you can stop them from perching on you.

Life desires run freely in our heart it is normal but you can stop them from making you anxious, panic and worry. The Lord says be anxious for nothing.

Uncontrol desires can lead to anxiety. Anxiety leads to worry. Worry leads to fear and fear is the beginning of evil steps.

Any steps taking in fear leads to death, error and regret.

- The truth of the matter is your word expresses your faith and/or your fear, **II Cor. 4:31**. You actually express what you fear or what you believe when you speak.

Rather than expressing doubt and fear, why not declare what God's word says: **Philippians 4: 19, Psalm 16: 6, Isaiah 65: 21** etc.

Finally, rather than worry why not pray about it first – **Philippians 4: 6.**

As I close this chapter, I like you to take a moment to pray about your worries.

START ITH THIS PRAYER

1. Lord I realised that I can't help the situation in my life now, I resolved to you today.

2. I submit my burdens, care and worries to you. Take my burdens and free me.

Chapter 4

DANGERS OF LOOSING A SOLID GRIP

Hebrews 10: 39 |

"But we are not of those who shrink back and are destroyed, but of those who believe and are saved."

When you lose your self-esteem for sitting way too long in loss of motivation, big problems will crept in to entangle you. One big target of the devil/enemy here is to get your soul. To get at you, he will push forward anything that can further discourage you. The final demon Satan uses to subject man into spiritual light out is secret. Many things will handcuff you in your closest such that you wouldn't want anyone to be aware of. Now from a moment of lingering to procrastination you have finally landed yourself in the net. Let's examine what happens to a person in Satan's net.

Common Demon that operates in the Closest of a self-motivationally dead person:

Note: "Satanic trap or net" is another term that refers to a situation in which a person becomes ensnared in a harmful or destructive lifestyle or belief system. Here are potential consequences of falling into a satanic trap:

1. ***Loss of moral compass***: A person caught in a satanic trap may begin to lose their sense of right and wrong, leading them to engage in behaviours that are harmful to themselves or others.

2. ***Loss of heaven:*** A home at last for all who gives up the way of evil and follow the way of God through faith in Jesus Christ.

3. ***Isolation***: The Satanic trap may lead a person to isolate themselves from friends and family members who could help them escape the trap, leaving them feeling alone and vulnerable.

4. ***Mental and emotional distress:*** Being caught in a satanic trap can cause significant mental and emotional distress, leading to anxiety, depression, and other mental health issues.

5. ***Spiritual emptiness:*** A person caught in a satanic trap may feel spiritually empty

and disconnected from their beliefs, leading to a sense of hopelessness and despair.

6. ***Prostituting and drug addiction:*** this is the worst phenomenon in the life of those caught up in satanic trap.

****

Now that you know that there is a reason behind these social vices going on in your life, I advise you to do the best to free yourself from Satan's trap today.

****

Ways to be Free from Addiction and Prostitutions:

Developing healthier habits can be a challenging but worthwhile process. Here are a few suggestions that may be helpful:

1. ***Seek professional help:*** Consider seeking the help of a therapist or counselor who specializes in addiction and can provide you with the support and guidance you need to overcome your struggles.

2. ***Join a support group:*** Consider joining a support group such as Narcotics Anonymous or Sex Addicts Anonymous. These groups can provide you with a community of people who understand what you are going through

and can offer you support and encouragement.

3. **Identify triggers:** Identify the situations, people, or emotions that trigger your urge to engage in prostitution or drug use. Once you have identified these triggers, you can develop strategies to avoid or manage them.
2 Thessalonians 3: 6 *"In the name of the Lord Jesus Christ, we command you, brothers, to keep away from every brother who is idle and does not live according to the teaching you received from us."*

4. **Develop healthy coping mechanisms:** Instead of turning to prostitution or drugs to cope with stress or difficult emotions, try to develop healthier coping mechanisms such as exercise, meditation, or spending time with supportive friends and family members. Above all, ill-gotten wealth has severe consequences. Money made from prostituting adds sorrows. Work with your own hands.

5. **Create a routine:** Establish a daily routine that includes healthy habits such as exercise, healthy eating, and getting enough sleep. This can help you feel more in control of your life and reduce your reliance on drugs or prostitution.

6. ***Join a bible class today***: Take regular part in bible teaching classes can help you overcome addiction and any other lording social vices in your life. The word of God helps in forming a new nature in man.

7. ***Consider Fasting and Prayer:*** listen to this one. Either you are a Christian, a Muslim or a Pagan to stop an evil thirst you must create a good thirst. To stop the evil hunger you must create a holy hunger: and to break a long time bad habits, try long days fasting. All habits are formed within 8 – 40 days. Decide to set that crucial time, when you cannot but indulge in your addiction, to fast and abstain from your addiction. Practice this for a period of 40 days. And attend bible class regularly; you will be amazed how you will turn out to be.

Remember, overcoming addiction and prostitution is a difficult process, but it is possible with the right support and tools. Don't be afraid to reach out for help and take it one day at a time.

==

Consequences of Loosing a Solid Grip

As Christians, it is important to maintain a solid grip on Jesus' salvation in order to make it to heaven. Losing our grip on salvation can have serious consequences, both in this life and in the life to come. Here are some dangers of losing a solid grip on Jesus' salvation, supported by relevant Bible verses:

1. Falling away from the faith.

When we lose our grip on Jesus' salvation, we run the risk of falling away from the faith altogether. In **Hebrews 6:4-6**, it is written, *"It is impossible for those who have once been enlightened, who have tasted the heavenly gift, who have shared in the Holy Spirit, who have tasted the goodness of the word of God and the powers of the coming age and who have fallen away, to be brought back to repentance."* This verse warns us that falling away from the faith after experiencing the goodness of God's salvation is a very serious matter.

2. Being deceived by false teachings.

When we are not firmly grounded in Jesus' salvation, we are more vulnerable to false teachings and doctrines. In **Colossians 2:8,** it is written, *"See to it that no one takes you captive through hollow and deceptive philosophy, which depends on human tradition and the elemental spiritual forces of* *this world rather than on Christ.*" This verse reminds us that false teachings can lead us astray from the truth of Jesus' salvation, and that we must be cautious and discerning in our spiritual journey.

3. Losing our hope and confidence in Christ.

When we lose our grip on Jesus' salvation, we may also lose our hope and confidence in Him. In **Hebrews 3:14**, it is written, "*We have come to share in Christ, if indeed we hold our original conviction firmly to the very end.*" This verse reminds us that our faith must be steadfast and unwavering in order to share in the fullness of Christ's salvation. Losing our grip on salvation can lead to doubt and uncertainty, which can ultimately lead us away from Christ.

4. Missing out on the blessings and rewards of salvation.

Finally, when we lose our grip on Jesus' salvation, we run the risk of missing out on the blessings and rewards that come with it. In **Revelation 3:11**, it is written, "*I am coming soon. Hold on to what you have, so that no one will take your crown.*" This verse reminds us that we must hold fast to Jesus' salvation in order to receive the fullness of the blessings and rewards

Chapter 5

HOW TO STAY MOTIVATED FOR GOOD WORKS?

As Christians, it is not uncommon to struggle with lukewarmness in our faith. We may find ourselves lacking motivation to engage in good works or to share the gospel with others. However, there are several things we can do to stay motivated and overcome lukewarmness. Here are some points to consider:

1. ***Remember your first love and renew your passion for Christ.***

In ***Revelation 2: 4 - 5,*** Jesus speaks to the church in Ephesus and says, "*Yet I hold this against you: You have forsaken the love you had at first. Consider how far you have fallen! Repent and do the things you did at first.*" This verse reminds us that we can become lukewarm when we lose sight of our first love for Christ. To overcome lukewarmness, it is important to renew our passion for Christ and to remember the joy and excitement we felt when we first encountered Him.

One way to do this is through prayer and worship. Spending time in prayer and worship can help us to refocus our hearts on Christ and to remember the depth of His love for us. It can also help us to gain a fresh perspective on our faith and to see the ways in which God is working in our lives.

2. *Seek fellowship with other believers.*

Another way to stay motivated in our faith is to seek fellowship with other believers. In **Hebrews 10: 24 - 25,** it is written, "*And let us consider how we may spur one another on toward love and good deeds, not giving up meeting together, as some are in the habit of doing, but encouraging one another.*" This verse reminds us that we are not meant to walk alone in our faith. By connecting with other believers, we can find encouragement, accountability, and support to help us stay motivated to our duty post and in our good works.

3. *Focus on the eternal rewards.*

In **1 Corinthians 15:58,** it is written, "*Therefore, my dear brothers and sisters, stand firm. Let nothing move you. Always give yourselves fully to the work of the Lord, because you know that your labor in the Lord is not in vain.*" This verse reminds us that our good works have eternal significance and that we will be rewarded for our faithfulness. By focusing on the eternal rewards, we can find motivation to continue in our good works, even when we feel discouraged or disheartened.

We suffer major setback today because our bosses are not praising us or someone is hijacking our rewards. I understand that it can be painful when you are not given credit for your hard labours but your boss is using your work to amass promotion and relevance. You may become frustrated and loose the motivation to continue in that office. But I will advise you to stay strong. They say nothing last forever. Although, that doesn't mean you should be stupid.

Speak up where you need to, appease your name and stamp duty where it's required but be wise and be prayerful. That's because what goes round comes around.

The point here is doing all that is assigned to you vigorously not for men but for a clear conscience and a good name. Your labour of love will never go unnoticed.

4. *Practice gratitude and cultivate a heart of thankfulness.*

Another way to stay motivated in our faith and career pursuits is to practice gratitude and cultivate a heart of thankfulness

Appreciate everyone in your life

Those who work with you and those giving you opportunity appreciate them always. You will be surprised to see them giving you more support and encouragement that will encourage you to do more.

FAQS

Q: What may help a Christian youth with great potential but a poor background succeeds in life?

Ans:

1. Trust in God: One of the most important things that a Christian youth can do is trust in God. The Bible teaches us that God is faithful and will provide for us. *"Trust in the Lord with all your heart and lean not on your own understanding; in all your ways submit to him, and he will make your paths straight."* (*Proverbs 3:5-6).*

2. **Work hard:** Hard work is essential for success, and the Bible encourages us to work hard. *"Whatever you do, work at it with all your heart, as working for the Lord, not for human masters."* *(Colossians 3:23).*

3. **Persevere**: Success is not always easy to come by, and it often requires perseverance. The Bible teaches us to persevere through difficult times. *"Consider it pure joy, my brothers and sisters, whenever you face trials of many kinds, because you know that the testing of your faith produces perseverance."* *(James 1:2-3).*

4. **Seek wisdom:** Wisdom is essential for success, and the Bible encourages us to seek wisdom. *"The fear of the Lord is the beginning of wisdom, and knowledge of the Holy One is understanding."* *(Proverbs 9:10).* Attend seminar and entrepreneurship development training etc.

5. **Seek guidance:** Seeking guidance from others who have gone before us can be helpful. The Bible encourages us to seek guidance from wise people. *"Listen to advice and accept discipline, and at the end you will* *be counted among the wise."* (**Proverbs 19:20**).

6.   Be humble: Humility is an important characteristic for success, and the Bible encourages us to be humble. *"Do nothing out of selfish ambition or vain conceit. Rather, in humility value others above yourselves."* (**Philippians   2:3**).   Humility   brings connection with people on the high table.

7.   Have   faith: Faith is essential for success, and the Bible teaches us to have faith in God. *"Now faith is confidence in what we hope for and assurance about what we do not see."* (**Hebrews 11:1**).

8.   Be grateful: Being grateful for what we have can help us to succeed, and the Bible encourages us to be grateful. *"Give thanks in all circumstances; for this is God's will for you in Christ Jesus."* (1 **Thessalonians 5: 18**.)

*****   *****   *****   *****

Q: What can a Family man/ head that is about to give up do to find motivation?

Ans: - Seek support from others, whether it is friends, family, or a professional counsellor. You don't have to go through this alone. (***Read Proverbs 11:14).***

- Take time to rest and recharge. It's okay to take a break and come back to the situation with a fresh perspective. (***Matthew 11:28-30***).

- Pray about it. Invite God to the situation and see a miracle of God.

- Remember why you started and focus on the positive aspects of your family and your role as a family head. ***(Philippians 4:8).*** Someone once told me to never start what I cannot continue.

***** ***** ***** *****

Q: Married woman that's fed up or loss interest in keeping her marriage, what can she do?

Answer:

- Communicate with your spouse about how you're feeling and work together to find a solution. (***Ephesians 4:26-27).***

- Seek guidance from a trusted mentor or counsellor. They can provide objective advice and help you work through your feelings. (**Proverbs 15:22).**

- Focus on the positive aspects of your marriage and try to rekindle the love and passion that brought you together in the first place. (**1 Corinthians 13:4-7**).

- Remember your children. Where two elephants fight the green plants suffer.

- Finally, try God. He instituted marriage and hate divorce. Pray about it.

***** ***** ***** *****

Q: What shall a business man/woman that loss the motivation needed to continue do?

Answer:

- Take a break and recharge. Sometimes stepping away from the situation can help you regain your motivation. **Isaiah 40:31 |** *"but those who hope in the LORD will renew their strength. They will soar on wings like eagles; they will run and not grow weary, they will walk and not be faint."*

- Set new goals and create a plan to achieve them. Having a clear direction and purpose can help reignite your passion. (**Proverbs 16:3**).

\- Seek inspiration from successful entrepreneurs or business leaders. Learn from their experiences and adopt their strategies. (***Proverbs 13:20***).

Happy are ye if you do these things.

Shalom!

About The Book

Inspiration fuels the wheel we ride to climb higher. This inspiration could be good or bad. We all have one everyday task above all; identify the source of pure and right inspiration. You must know where to draw your inspiration from.

Should you loose focus and find it difficult to draw inspiration from the right source, you will surfer death of self-motivation. The inspiration gotten from the right or wrong source provokes you into action either good or bad.

This book in its simplicity provides a self help to revive the spirituality, self-motivation and the will of continuity in Jesus and good works.

The book leaves you with a rhetorical question, where do you draw your strength from?

About the Author

Oluyemi Stephen Beloved is a Christian author, a preacher and a discipler.

He has authored few books that people are talking about in many nations of the world today. If you Google his name you will see it too.

He is a practical man, married with kids.